BUYER BEWARE!

A guide to finding out about contaminated land

CONTENTS

Friends of the Earth

BUYER BEWARE!

A guide to finding out about contaminated land

BUYER BEWARE!

A guide to finding out about contaminated land

Written and researched by: **Benedict Southworth, Mike Childs** *York Friends of the Earth*, Tim Treuherz *Manchester Friends of the Earth*
Editors: **Benedict Southworth, Sarah Finch**
Book Design: **David Caines**
Cover photos: **Phototake/ACE, Paul Thompson/ACE**

This publication has been partially funded by the London Boroughs Grants Committee.

Friends of the Earth

Friends of the Earth is one of the UK's leading environmental groups. It works locally, nationally and internationally and provides authoritative information on a wide range of international issues. It has an active network of over 300 Local Groups.

Friends of the Earth is backed by more than 215,000 supporters in the UK. For information on how to join, or your nearest Local Group, or for a free copy of our publications or merchandise catalogue, please write to: Friends of the Earth, 56-58 Alma Street, Luton, Beds LU1 2YZ, enclosing a stamped addressed envelope.

July 1993
© Friends of the Earth
Published by Friends of the Earth Trust Limited
ISBN 1 85750 206 X

Friends of the Earth
Friends of the Earth
26-28 Underwood Street
London N1 7JQ
(071) 490 1555

Friends of the Earth Scotland
Bonnington Mill
70-72 Newhaven Road
Edinburgh EH6 5QG

LONDON
BOROUGHS
GRANTS
COMMITTEE

1. What is contaminated land?

Chemicals left behind in the soil by a wide range of industrial activities can damage the environment and pose threats to people's health and property. There are an estimated 100,000 contaminated sites in the UK, a legacy of years of polluting land uses.

Table 1 below shows the major sources of soil contamination. A fuller list is given in Appendix 1.

Table 1: Causes of contaminated land. The table gives the proportion of the total number of contaminated sites caused by each activity, not of the total area covered.	
Gas Works	25.8 %
Waste tips	25.8 %
Metal Industries	9.0 %
Sewage works/sludge tips	7.8 %
Chemical works	7.4 %
Docks and wharfs	4.1 %
Tar, oil, petroleum depots	3.3 %
Scrap Yards	3.1 %
Munitions	1.2 %
Tanneries	1.0 %
Other	11.5%
[Reference: Figures presented to a Parliamentary Inquiry in 1989 by the Interdepartmental Committee on the Redevelopment of Contaminated Land (ICRCL)]	

Hazards associated with contaminated land

Land can be contaminated with a wide range of different chemicals. Appendix 2 outlines some of the contaminants commonly associated with some land uses, but the contamination present will vary depending on the exact nature and use of the site itself.

Problems associated with contaminated land may include:

Hazards to human health: many of the pollutants found in contaminated land are poisonous or suspected of causing cancer. Some of these chemicals can pass through the skin so people can be exposed to contamination through direct contact with the soil. Small children often eat soil or put objects in their mouth so they can be at particular risk from contaminated land. Some chemicals may be contained in dust blown from contaminated sites so there may be a risk of inhaling particular materials.

Hazards to Water: groundwater used for public drinking water supplies can be polluted by contaminated land and is very expensive to clean up. Groundwaters provide a third of drinking water in England and Wales and seventy per cent in the south of England. Contaminated land can also pollute rivers and streams causing damage to wildlife.

Hazards to plants: many pollutants are toxic to plants and can create wastelands devoid of vegetation (although a lack of nutrients can create a similar effect). Other pollutants may be taken up by plants, passing into the food chain and posing a hazard to human health.

Gas generation: some pollutants may generate toxic or flammable gases. These gases can migrate away from the sites into nearby properties, causing explosions. Methane, a gas generated in waste disposal sites, is a powerful 'greenhouse gas' and contributes to the threat of climate change.

Danger to buildings: some pollutants can attack building materials, pipes and cables. This can lead to structural damage as well as pollution of water supplies.

Fire hazard: many industrial pollutants are potentially combustible, and may ignite through self heating or the proximity of power cables or surface fires. These fires, which can be difficult to put out, can produce toxic gases.

Caveat emptor: buyer beware!

At present the sale of contaminated land operates upon the principle of "caveat emptor" or "let the buyer beware". This means that individuals, local authorities or companies may purchase property on a contaminated site without being aware of the potential hazards and liabilities. The House of Commons Environment Committee recommended that the Government should introduce legislation *"to place upon vendors a duty to declare information in their possession about contamination present on site, however caused"* but the Government has so far failed to do this. This means that it is up to you to find out about the contamination of any land you want to buy.

Plans to build up to 2,000 homes on land near Chatham had to be halted after the site was found to be heavily contaminated with heavy metals and blue asbestos. Originally thought to be virgin agricultural land, it turned out to be part of the former Chatham Naval Dockyard. The developers were forced to spend nearly £30 million pounds cleaning up the site before building could be started.

Above: More than 1,000 people live on or nearby contaminated land in estates in Greenwich, London. Their homes were built on a filled-in rubbish tip. Residents only began to suspect that there might be a problem when 'blue blotches' appeared in their gardens. The Council has now fenced off part of the site, put up warning signs and covered the residents gardens with a strong plastic sheet and clean topsoil. Many residents are unhappy about the potential risk to their own and their children's health.

Above: The Church Milton estate in Sittingbourne, Kent was built on a site contaminated by toxic metals from buried rubbish. When the contamination came to light, children living on the estate were tested for blood lead levels. Parents were advised to cover soil in their gardens with plastic sheeting or another barrier and to ensure that children washed their hands thoroughly after playing outside.

2. Finding out about contaminated land in your area

In some cases it is easy to see that a site may be potentially contaminated. In others - where land has been redeveloped - it is more difficult. But redeveloped land may still be highly contaminated and may pose a real risk to people and the environment. There are a number of different ways in which you can start an investigation. You will need to be something of a detective. The following sections outline some of the possible sources of information on contaminated land. It is likely that you will get only partial information from one source so you will have to compare the information you get from any one source with that from another.

Edmund Campion Southworth

Above: In some cases it is easy to see that a site may be contaminated by industrial use. When the site is redeveloped it may be more difficult.

Local authorities

Some local authorities will have information on potentially contaminated land within their areas. Your first step should be to contact the County and District Councils and ask what investigations have been carried out and if you can have the results. To find out if your council has prepared a report on contaminated land write a letter to the Chief Environmental Health Officer or the Chief Planning Officer. These reports can be either general or about particular sites.

A good source of information from the County Council will be the *Derelict and Despoiled Land Survey*. This survey identifies a large number of sites but gives limited information on each one. Also, by definition, it does not contain information on sites that have been redeveloped.

The Cambridge Water Company was forced to close a drinking water borehole after it was found to be contaminated with tetrachloroethene, a chlorinated solvent, at levels 200 times above the legal standards for drinking water. The pollution was traced to a tannery run by Eastern Counties Leathers. Cambridge Water Company is taking legal action to recover the £1 million it spent on providing a replacement supply.

Waste Regulatory Authorities (County Councils in England, District Councils in Wales, Department of the Environment in Northern Ireland) hold public registers of all waste disposal site licences issued since 1976. This register can be used to locate sites, open and closed, within your area. The Waste Regulatory Authorities may also have information on sites which were closed before site licences were introduced.

County Councils (Fire and Civil Defence Authorities in Metropolitan areas) are responsible for controlling all premises which store petroleum. They keep a register of licences, which should contain information about the location of the sites and the controls on storage and monitoring.

Other sources of information

If the information from local government is incomplete or unavailable then you will have to look at other sources. The most likely sources are described below.

Maps

One of the main sources of information about the location of sites polluted by past industrial activity is old maps. These tend to provide more information than modern maps would about a particular site.

The county maps described below should be available in the Central Library for your area. However not all the maps will be available or complete. The National Map Library (part of the British Library, in London) has a near complete set of maps and is open to the public.

57 families were evacuated from a housing estate in Portsmouth. The families were given 24 hours to leave their homes after dangerous levels of asbestos were found in air and soil samples. The houses had been built on a former Ministry of Defence landfill site. The landfill had been covered with clean topsoil to prevent contamination but the capping proved inadequate.

The maps that are likely to be of greatest use are:

■ *County Series 6" maps* (six inches to a mile)
These are good for identifying large industrial sites. In rural and semi-rural areas they will show at least 95 per cent of industrial sites. Apart from those in the inner cities, sites are labelled with the type of industrial use for example 'gasworks',

'waste tip'. Figure 1 shows an example of a county series 6"
map.

■ *County Series 25" maps* (25 inches to a mile)
These can be used for identifying larger industrial sites within
a city. Again, these sites are usually labelled with a
description of the industrial use. These maps were compiled
until 1938.

The site of an old
chemical factory in
Ilford was found to
have radioactive
'hotspots' 50 times
the normal
background level. The
radiation, found by
the Friends of the
Earth Radiation
Monitoring Unit, is
from thorium which
was dumped on the
soil when the factory
was in use. Thorium
decomposes to
radioactive radon gas
which if inhaled can
lead to lung cancer.

■ *1:10,000 Ordnance Survey maps*
(six inches to a mile)
These are useful for locating former
industrial sites. Different types of site
are not identifed but are all marked
as 'works' or 'factories'. These maps
were compiled from 1955.

The following maps may also be
useful but are generally less help
than those above.

1:500 town maps (one hundred and
twenty inches to a mile)
Only one edition of these maps was
completed, some time in the late
1800s. They provide very detailed
information but are difficult to get
hold of locally.

1:2,500 Ordnance Survey maps
(twenty four inches to a mile)
These contain information similar to
that on 1:10,000 maps, however not
all areas have been covered.

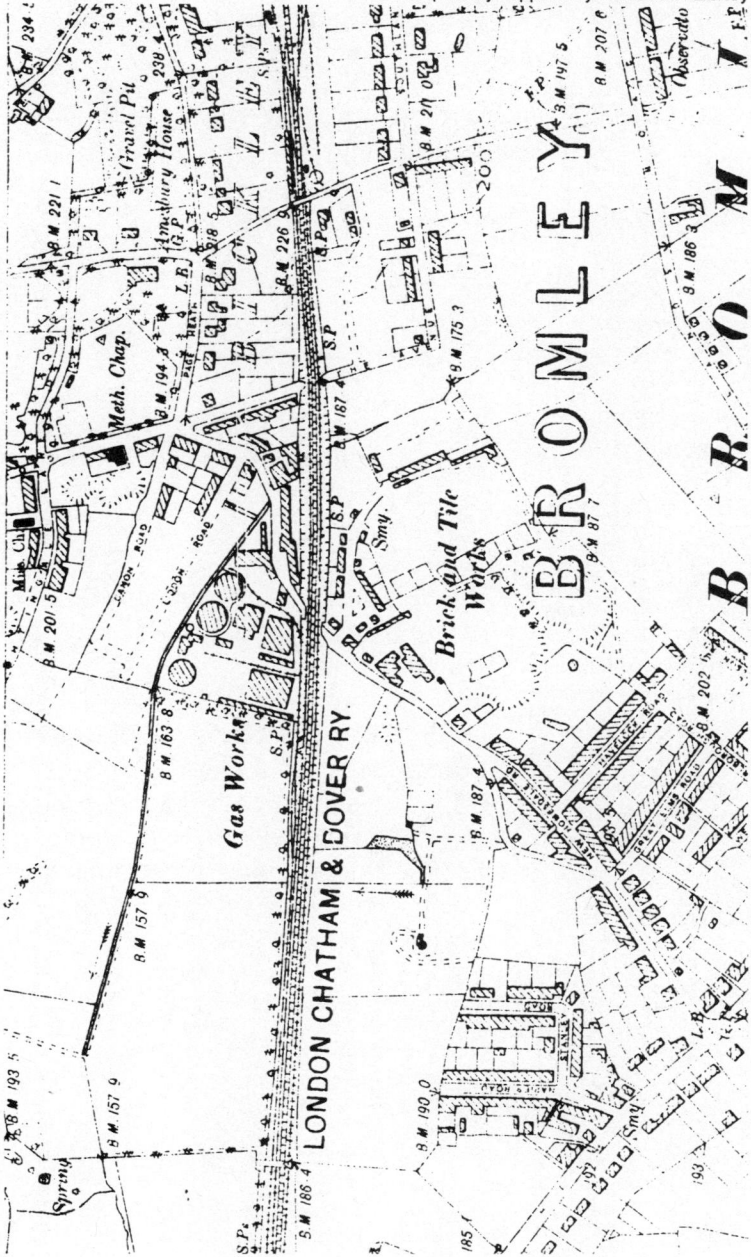

Figure 1: This map of Bromley in 1898 from the 6" County Series clearly shows the location of a gas works and a brick and tile works.

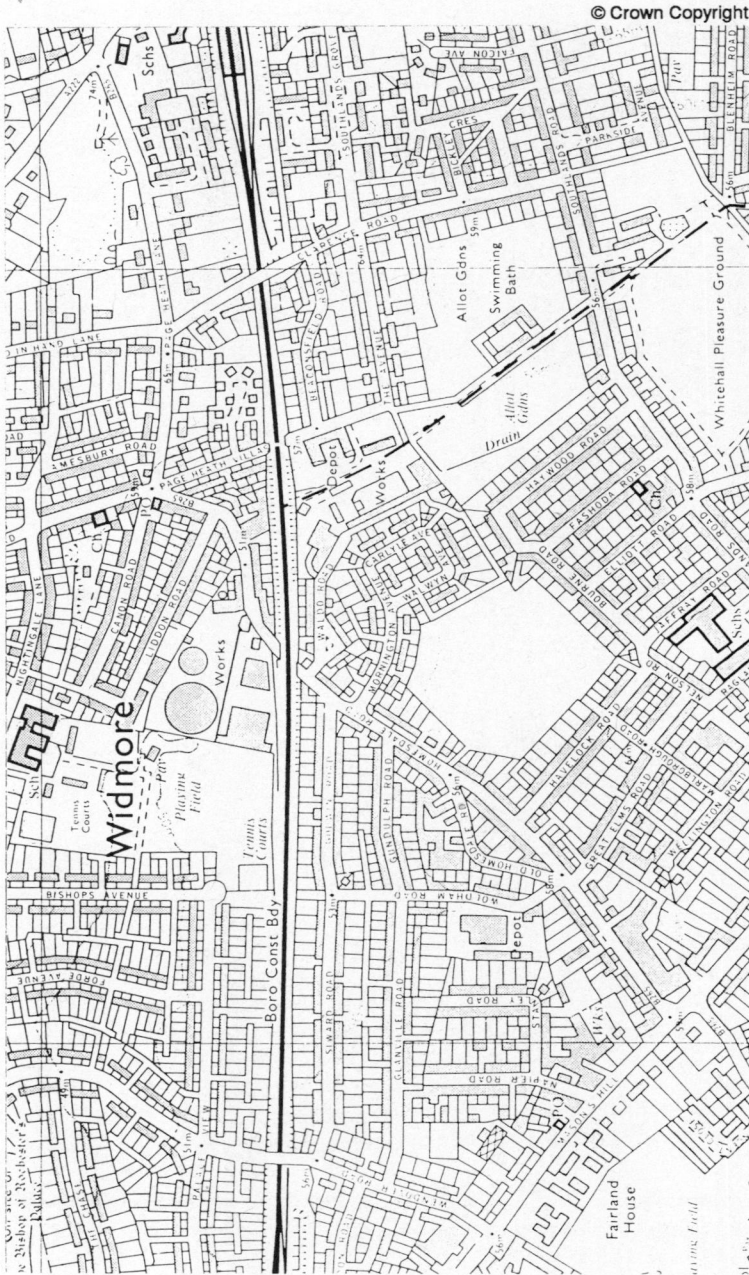

© Crown Copyright

Figure 2: On the 1975 map, the brick and tile works has disappeared and houses have been built on the site.

Trade directories

From the mid-eighteenth century until the 1930s local directories were published containing commercial information including the names and addresses. This makes them useful if you want to check a particular trade or process.

The best known of these were the Kelly's Directories published in County or City volumes between 1799 and 1939. These and other directories are available from libraries and record offices.

facsimile

ELECTRO PLATERS & GILDERS

(See also Electro Plate Manufacturers)

Adams & Co. East Stanley st. Blackfriars rd. S

BAXENDALE & CO. LIMITED, Miller st.

Biddulph & Co. electro-plating and enamel-
ling, 18 - 30 Linnard st **TN City 2,551**

Brailey & Co, 36 Albert st

BRAILEY & WISEMAN, Lion Works,
Little Peter st

Brown Herbert Stanley, 11A Sugar la

Brunner Brothers, 22 Oxford rd. C on M

Brunner L. & Co. 308 Queen's rd. M P

Buss John R. & Sons, Ltd. 64 and 66 King st

City Electro Plating Co. 22 Chester rd. H

COMMERCIAL PLATING COMPANY (THE), Blantyre st. H

T N Central 5,186;

T A "PLATINCO, Blantyre Street"

Above: The 1930 edition of Kelly's Directory for the Manchester area lists the location of potentially polluting industrial premises which might have been redeveloped.

Below: The 1930 edition of Kelly's Directory

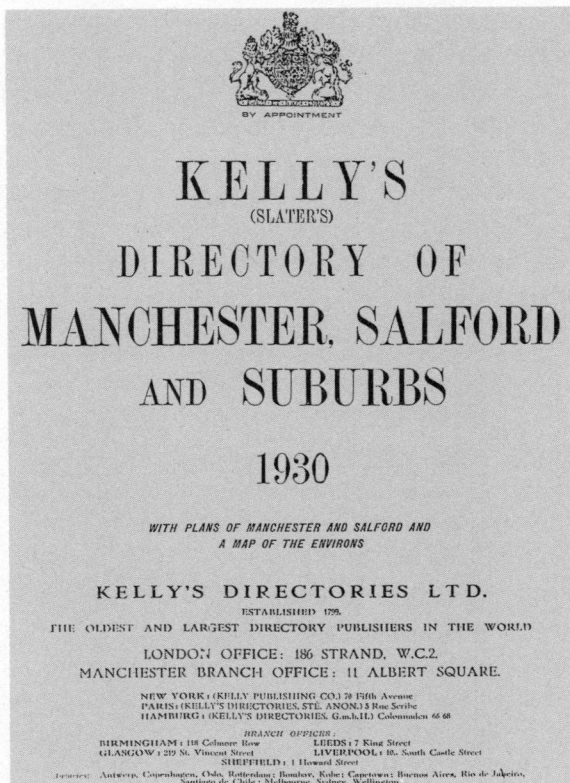

BY APPOINTMENT

KELLY'S
(SLATER'S)

DIRECTORY OF
MANCHESTER, SALFORD
AND SUBURBS

1930

WITH PLANS OF MANCHESTER AND SALFORD AND
A MAP OF THE ENVIRONS

KELLY'S DIRECTORIES LTD.

ESTABLISHED 1799.
THE OLDEST AND LARGEST DIRECTORY PUBLISHERS IN THE WORLD

LONDON OFFICE: 186 STRAND, W.C.2.
MANCHESTER BRANCH OFFICE: 11 ALBERT SQUARE.

NEW YORK: (KELLY PUBLISHING CO.) 20 Fifth Avenue
PARIS: (KELLY'S DIRECTORIES, STÉ. ANON.) 5 Rue Scribe
HAMBURG: (KELLY'S DIRECTORIES, G.m.b.H.) Colonnaden 66-68

BRANCH OFFICES:
BIRMINGHAM: 118 Colmore Row   LEEDS: 7 King Street
GLASGOW: 219 St. Vincent Street   LIVERPOOL: 10, South Castle Street
SHEFFIELD: 1 Howard Street

Agencies: Antwerp, Copenhagen, Oslo, Rotterdam; Bombay, Kobe; Capetown; Buenos Aires, Rio de Janeiro, Santiago de Chile; Melbourne, Sydney, Wellington

Local archives and histories
Local history libraries and county record offices hold local archive collections, business histories and personal papers. These can provide a wealth of information on the history of an area.

Local Archeological and Historical Societies also hold a wide range of information. The local library may have autobiographies, biographies and the results of local oral history projects which may contain references to sites that have now disappeared.

BUYER BEWARE!

These sources are useful primarily for cross-checking information from other sources.

Not all the clues to the location of potentially contaminated land will be in obvious places. Even looking through a modern A-Z can be useful. Foundry Lane is an obvious example of a street name which might point to the old usage. A search of the Greater Manchester area revealed seven Gas Streets.

Her Majesty's Inspectorate of Pollution (HMIP)
HMIP holds information previously held by the Alkali Inspectorate. This will apply mainly to the chemical and large industrial sectors.

Your right to environmental information

Much of the information mentioned above is already available to the public through local libraries or public registers. However, people sometimes experience difficulties in getting hold of information on pollution problems. A new law which came into force on January 1st 1993, and the Government's stated commitment to citizen's rights to information, should make things easier.

Friends of the Earth groups around the UK have conducted surveys into the locations of potentially contaminated sites.

A study by Friends of the Earth Cymru found 968 potentially contaminated sites in Wales. The study combined data from the Welsh Office with information about landfill sites and used the latest computer technology to map the information. The cost of cleaning up the Welsh sites has been put as high as £8bn.

A survey by Friends of the Earth in London found 68 sites which were previously used for the production of town gas. At least 30 of the sites have been partially or completely redeveloped - the new uses include a DIY centre, two supermarkets and the headquarters of the Department of the Environment.

The Environmental Information Regulations 1992 guarantee members of the public access to environmental information - such as the results of testing for contaminated land - held by public bodies.

Requests for information made under the Regulations must be specific and in writing. The public authorities have to respond to all requests within two months, either by providing the information or giving a reason why the request is being refused. Information can be refused on the grounds of commercial confidentiality, when work is still in progress or when it contains personal information. The provider of the information can charge for the administrative costs of your request, so it is advisable to ask for an estimate of the cost with your request.

Friends of the Earth Northern Ireland conducted a similar survey and found 18 former gas works sites. Five of these sites were unknown to the local borough councils.

The Local Government (Access to Information) Act 1985 gives you the right to inspect and make copies of council reports and the background documents used to make the report. The Council can make a charge for inspecting background papers but not the report.

The Government's *Citizens' Charter* states that the public should be able to find out about contaminated land from their local authority and you can use it to put pressure on the Council to give you information.

The main council office will have a list of your rights to information which is available on request. Copies of all the regulations mentioned in this book are available from Her Majesty's Stationery Office. The Citizens Charter is available from the Department of the Environment.

Friends of the Earth groups in Banbury, York and the Vale of Evesham have also sleuthed out the whereabouts of contaminated sites in their areas.

3. Measuring and cleaning up contaminated land

Measuring contamination

Once you have found out that, for instance, your home, school or shopping centre is on land which might be contaminated from past use you will want to find out how much contamination is actually there.

A number of different bodies have responsibility for monitoring for different types of contamination. You can ask them for information about their findings and ask to see their monitoring data.

District Councils
If the District Council has been investigating the whereabouts of contaminated sites it may have also been monitoring them.

If you are worried that an area of land may be contaminated you can ask the Environmental Health Department to carry out some monitoring. Appendix 2 should give you an idea of what the council should be looking for.

County Councils
The Waste Regulatory Authorities monitor for pollution problems at open and closed landfill sites in the county and you can gain access to the monitoring results.

National Rivers Authority
The National Rivers Authority (NRA) is responsible for protecting the water environment in England and Wales (in Northern Ireland the Department of the Environment is responsible). One of the NRA's duties is to monitor the quality of river water, groundwater and coastal waters. The NRA may

well have been monitoring contaminated land in your area, for example, in the Severn Trent region the NRA has identified over 200 contaminated sites which threaten to pollute water.

The information obtained by the NRA is held on a public register, which you can look at free of charge. You will find the number for your nearest NRA office in the telephone directory.

Urban Development Corporations
In some areas the Urban Development Corporations will have records of contaminated land in their area and the results of monitoring.

Cleaning up contaminated land

Through a body called the Interdepartmental Committee on the Redevelopment of Contaminated Land (ICRCL) the Government has set 'acceptable' levels of pollutants in land that is being brought into redevelopment. These guidelines are used to judge whether the levels of contamination found pose a threat.

The guidelines are set at two levels:

'Threshold trigger levels' are defined as the concentration at which the contaminant becomes significant. However, the ICRCL notes state that *"even [if] the threshold trigger concentration is exceeded, this ought not to be taken automatically to mean that remedial action is essential".*

'Action trigger levels' are defined as levels at which the contaminant is considered undesirable or even unacceptable. If action trigger levels are exceeded then *"remedial action of some kind ... is then automatically required".*

The guidelines are set with reference to the end use, so the 'acceptable' levels of pollutants are higher for a car park than for other uses. The levels within the guidelines cover a relatively small number of pollutants. The guidelines are not statutory and they are not legally enforceable.

Some European countries have tougher laws on cleaning up contaminated land. Appendix 3 shows the ICRCL guidelines and the limits set by the Netherlands government for comparison. You will see that there is a significant difference in the numbers of pollutants looked at in the two countries.

The Netherlands guidelines have been used by some other European countries as the starting point for developing their own schemes.

Paying for the clean up

The cost of cleaning up the UK's contaminated land has been estimated at £10-30 billion. At present, this cost falls upon local authorities or developers.

Local authorities may apply for permission to borrow money in the form of Supplementary Credit Approvals (SCAs) to pay for cleaning up contaminated land. The total SCAs available for this purpose and controlling landfill gas have been cut from £25 million last year to £12 million in 1993. The cost of cleaning up sites is likely to be much higher, for example the Dutch spent £100 million on cleaning up one 8 hectare gasworks site in the centre of Utrecht.

Derelict Land Grants are available to those other than local authorities, for example private firms and individuals, nationalised industries, charitable trusts and parish councils. The grant pays 80 per cent of costs in Assisted Areas and

Derelict Land Clearance Areas and 50 per cent elsewhere. A total of £87.9 million was available in 1991/92.

The National Rivers Authority has the power to clean up any contaminated land which is polluting rivers, streams, and underground waters. It can then recover its costs from the land owner. However the NRA has yet to exercise this power.

Appendix 1. A list of potentially contaminating land uses

■ AGRICULTURE

Burial of diseased livestock

■ EXTRACTIVE INDUSTRY

Extracting, handling and storage of carbonaceous materials such as coal, lignite, petroleum, natural gas, or bituminous shale (not including the underground working)

Extracting, handling and storage of ores and their constituents.

■ ENERGY INDUSTRY

Producing gas from coal, lignite, oil or other carbonaceous material (other than from sewage or other waste), or from mixtures of those materials

Reforming, refining, purifying and odourizing natural gas or any product of the processes outlined in C.3.a) above.

Pyrolysis, carbonization, distillation, liquefaction, partical, oxidation, other heat treatment, conversation, purification, or refining of coal, lignite, oil, other carbonaceous material or mixtures and products thereof, otherwise than with a view to gasification or making of charcoal.

A thermal power station (including nuclear power stations and production, enrichment and reprocessing of nuclear fuels).

Electricity sub-station.

■ PRODUCTION OF METALS

Production, refining or recovery of metals by physical, chemical, thermal or electrolytic or other extraction process.

Heating, melting or casting metals as part of an intermediate or final manufacturing process (including annealing, tempering or similar processes).

Cold forming processes (including pressing, rolling, extruding, stamping, forming or similar processes).

Finishing treatments, including anodizing, pickling, coating, and plating or similar processes.

■ PRODUCTION OF NON-METALS AND THEIR PRODUCTS

Production or refining of non-metals by treatment of the ore.

Production or processing of mineral fibres by treatment of the ore.

Cement, lime and gypsum manufacture, brickworks and associated processes.

■ GLASS MAKING AND CERAMICS

Manufacture of glass and products based on glass.

Manufacture of ceramics and products based on ceramics, including glazes and vitreous enamel.

■ PRODUCTION AND USE OF CHEMICALS

Production, refining, recovery or storage of petroleum or petrochemicals or their by-products, including tar and bitumen processes and manufacture of asphalt.

Production, refining and bulk storage of organic or inorganic chemicals, including fertilisers, pesticides, pharmaceuticals, soaps, detergents, cosmetics, toiletries, dyestuffs, inks, paints, fireworks, pyrotechnic materials or recovered chemicals.

Production, refining and bulk storage of industrial gases not otherwise covered.

■ ENGINEERING AND MANUFACTURING PROCESSES

Manufacture of metal goods, including mechanical engineering industrial plant or steelwork, motor vehicles, ships, railway or tramway vehicles, aircraft, aerospace equipment or similar equipment.

Storage, manufacture or testing of explosives, propellants, ordnance, small arms or ammunition.

Manufacture and repair of electrical and electronic components and equipment.

■ FOOD PROCESSING INDUSTRY

Manufacture of pet foods or animal feedstuffs.

Processing of animal by-products (including rendering of maggot farming, but excluding slaughterhouses, butchering).

■ PAPER, PULP AND PRINTING INDUSTRY

Making of paper pulp, paper of board, or paper or board products, including printing or de-inking.

■ TIMBER AND TIMBER PRODUCTS INDUSTRY

Chemical treatment and coating of timber and timber products.

■ TEXTILE INDUSTRY

Tanning, dressing, fellmongering or other process for preparing, treating or working leather.

Fulling, bleaching, dyeing or finishing fabrics or fibres.

Manufacture of carpets or other textile floor coverings (including linoleum works).

■ RUBBER INDUSTRY

Processing of natural or synthetic rubber (including tyre manufacture or retreading).

■ INFRASTRUCTURE

Marshalling, dismantling, repairing or maintenance or railway rolling stock.

Dismantling, repairing or maintenance of marine vessels, including Hovercraft.

Dismantling, repairing or maintenance of road transport or road haulage vehicles.

Dismantling, repairing or maintenance of air or space transport systems.

■ WASTE DISPOSAL

Treating of sewage or other effluent.

Storage, treatment of disposal of sludge including sludge from water treatment works.

Treating, keeping, depositing or disposing of waste, including scrap (to include infilled canal basins, docks or rivercourses).

Storage or disposal of radioactive materials.

Laboratories for educational or research purposes.

The demolition of buildings, plant or equipment used for any of the activities in this list.

[Reference: Public Registers of Land which might be contaminated - A consultation Paper. May 1991]

Appendix 2. The possible contaminants associated with particular land uses

NB: Hydrocarbons, polychlorinated biphenyls (PCBs), asbestos, sulphates and many metals may be found on almost any site.

■ GAS WORK SITES

Before natural gas came on stream, town gas was manufactured using coal. There are an estimated 3,000-4,000 old town gas work sites in the U.K.

Town gas sites may be contaminated with:

- ■ Coal Tar
- ■ Phenols
- ■ Cyanides
- ■ Sulphur Compounds
- ■ Asbestos
- ■ Combustible substances
(eg coal and coke dusts)

■ LANDFILL SITES

There are over 6,000 currently operating landfill sites in the UK and up to 5,000 closed sites. Landfills generate a toxic cocktail of liquids (leachate) and landfill gas which contains the explosive gas methane. Methane also contributes to the threat of global climate change.

Landfill sites may be contaminated with:

- Metals including copper, zinc and lead
- Chlorinated industrial chemicals
- Asbestos
- Gases (eg methane)
- Leachates

■ METAL INDUSTRIES

There are literally thousands of metal industry premises within the UK. These include; mines, foundries, smelters, electroplating, engineering works and ship building yards.

Metal industry sites may be contaminated with:

- Metals especially iron, copper, nickel, chromium, zinc, cadmium, lead and asbestos

■ SEWAGE WORKS AND SLUDGE TIPS

The majority of liquid industrial waste in the UK is discharged through sewers. The waste then ends up at a sewage works. Most sewage works are not designed to deal with industrial waste and the pollutants either ends up in the sewage effluent or sludge. This means that old sewage works or sludge tips may contain a wide range of toxic metals.

Sewage works sites may be contaminated with:

- Metals (in sludges) including copper, nickel, lead, zinc, cadmium and mercury
- Micro organisms
- Organochlorine pesticides

■ CHEMICAL WORKS

There are at least 5,000 chemical works in the UK. It is almost impossible to discover which chemicals are being actively used, or have been used, at a specific site.

Chemical works may be contaminated with:

- ■ Acids
- ■ Alkalies
- ■ Metals
- ■ Solvents, e.g toluene, benzene
- ■ Phenols
- ■ Specialized organic compounds

■ DOCKS AND WHARFS

Docks and Wharfs can be contaminated with:

- ■ Metals
- ■ Organic compounds
- ■ Methane
- ■ Asbestos
- ■ Micro-organisms
- ■ Toxic, flammable or explosive substances

■ TAR, OIL AND PETROLEUM DEPOTS
(including petrol filling stations)

It is estimated that there may be as many as 10,000 leaking underground storage tanks just from the petrol distribution industy.

Tar, oil and petroleum depots can be contaminated with:

- Hydrocarbons
- Phenols
- Acids
- Alkalis
- Asbestos

■ SCRAP YARDS

Scrap yards can be contaminated with:

- Iron
- Copper
- Nickel
- Chromium
- Zinc
- Cadmium
- Lead
- Asbestos

■ TANNERIES

Tanneries pose a risk of water pollution and to people through the ingestion of soils or waters.

Tanneries can be contaminated with:

- Metals
- Arsenic
- Organic compounds

■ RAILWAY SIDINGS AND DEPOTS

Railway sidings can be contaminated with:

- ■ Hydrocarbons
- ■ Asbestos
- ■ Combustible substances

[Reference: British Standards Institute - Draft Code of practice for the identification of potentially contaminated land and its investigation. 1988]

Appendix 3. Guidelines for cleaning up contaminated land

Table i) UK Guidelines

The Interdepartmental Committee on the Redevelopment of Contaminated Land has set tentative *"trigger concentrations"* for the substances below. The levels are dependent on the type of land use and the future development of the site.

[NB The figures are presented for reference purposes only. For any practical applications they must be used in conjunction with the relevant footnotes and conditions laid out in the original table (see reference).]

Name of Substance		Threshold Level	Action Level
Acidity (PH less than)	Domestic gardens, allotments, landscaped areas	ph5	ph3
	Buildings, hard cover	NL	NL
Arsenic (As)	Domestic Gardens, allotments	10 mg/kg	
	Parks, playing fields, open space		
Boron (water-soluble)	Any uses where plants are to be grown	3 mg/kg	
Cadmium (Cd)	Domestic Gardens, allotments	3 mg/kg	
	Parks, playing fields, open space		
Chromium (Cr)	Domestic Gardens, allotments	600 mg/kg	
	Parks, playing fields, open space		
Copper (Cu)	Any uses where plants are to be grown	130 mg/kg	
Cyanide (CN as total complex)	Domestic Gardens, allotments	250 mg/kg	1000 mg/kg
	Landscaped areas	250 mg/kg	5000 mg/kg
	Buildings, hard cover	250 mg/kg	NL
Cyanide (CN as total free)	Domestic Gardens, allotments, landscaped areas	25 mg/kg	500 mg/kg
	Buildings, hard cover	100 mg/kg	500 mg/kg

Contaminant	Use		
Lead (Pb)	Domestic Gardens, allotments	500 mg/kg	
	Parks, playing fields, open space		
Mercury (Hg)	Domestic Gardens, allotments	1 mg/kg	
	Parks, playing fields, open space		
Nickel (Ni)	Any uses where plants are to be grown	70 mg/kg	
Phenols	Domestic Gardens, allotments	5 mg/kg	200 mg/kg
	Landscaped areas, buildings, hard covers	5 mg/kg	1000 mg/kg
Polyaromatic hydrocarbons	Domestic gardens, allotments, play areas	50 mg/kg	500 mg/kg
	Landscaped areas, buildings, hard cover	1000 mg/kg	10000 mg/kg
Selenium	Domestic Gardens, allotments	3 mg/kg	
	Parks, playing fields, open space		
Sulphate	Domestic gardens, allotments, landscaped areas	2000 mg/kg	10000 mg/kg
	Buildings	2000 mg/kg	
	Hard cover	5000 mg/kg	
Sulphur (S)	All proposed uses	50 mg/kg	50000 mg/kg
Thiocyanate(2)	All proposed uses	300 mg/kg	NL
Zinc (Zn)	Any uses where plants are to be grown	20000 mg/kg	NL

Table ii) Netherlands 'ABC' values

Name of Substance	Concentration in Soil			Concentration in Water		
	A	B	C	A	B	C
Metals						
Chromium (Cr)	100	250	800	20	50	200
Cobalt (Co)	20	50	300	20	50	200
Nickel (Ni)	50	100	500	20	50	200
Copper (Cu)	50	100	500	20	50	200
Zinc (Zn)	200	500	3000	50	200	800
Arsenic (As)	20	30	50	10	30	100
Molybdenum (Mo)	10	40	200	5	20	100
Cadmium (Cd)	1	5	20	1	2.5	10
Tin (Sn)	20	50	300	10	30	150
Barium (Ba)	200	400	2000	50	100	500
Mercury (Hg)	0.5	2	10	0.2	0.5	2
Lead (Pb)	50	150	600	20	50	200
Inorganic pollutants						
Ammonia (NH as N)	200	400	2000	200	1000	3000
Fluorine (F)	1	10	100	300	1200	4000
Cyanide (CN as total free)	5	50	500	5	30	100
Cyanide (CN as total complex)	2	20	200	10	50	200
Sulphur (S)				10	100	300
Bromine (Br)	20	50	300	100	500	2000
Phosphate (PO)				50	200	700

A = reference value below which soils are probably uncontaminated.
B = value above which there is need for further investigation.
C = value above which a clean-up is indicated.

BUYER BEWARE!

Category	Compound						
Aromatic compounds	Benzene	0.01	0.5	5	0.2	1	5
	Ethyl benzene	0.05	5	50	0.5	20	60
	Toluene	0.05	3	30	0.5	15	50
	Xylene	0.05	5	50	0.5	20	60
	Phenols	0.02	1	10	0.5	15	50
	Aromatics (total)	0.1	7	70	1	30	100
Polycyclic aromatic compounds	Napthalene	0.1	5	50	0.2	7	30
	Anthracene	0.1	10	100	0.1	2	10
	Phenanthrene	0.1	10	100	0.1	2	10
	Fluoranthene	0.1	10	100	0.02	1	5
	Pyrene	0.1	10	100	0.02	1	5
	Benzo(a)pyrene	0.05	1	10	0.01	0.2	1
	Total PCAs	1	20	200	0.2	10	40
Chlorinated organic compounds	Aliphatic chlorinated compounds (individual)	0.1	5	50	1	10	50
	Aliphatic chlorinated compounds (total)	0.1	7	70	1	15	70
	Chlorobenzenes (individual)	0.05	1	10	0.02	0.5	2
	Chlorobenzenes (total)	0.05	2	20	0.02	1	5
	Chlorophenols (individual)	0.01	0.5	5	0.01	0.3	1.5
	Chlorophenols (total)	0.01	1	10	0.01	0.5	2
	Chlorinated PCA (total)	0.05	1	10	0.01	0.2	1

Pesticides	PCB (total)	0.05	1	10	0.01	0.2	1
	EOCl (total)	0.1	8	80	1	15	70
	Organic Chlorinated pesticides (individual)	0.1	0.5	5	0.05	0.2	1
	Organic Chlorinated pesticides (total)	0.1	1	10	0.1	0.5	2
Other pollutants	Pesticides (total)	0.1	2	20	0.1	1	5
	Tetrahydrofuran	0.1	4	40	0.5	20	60
	Pyridine	0.1	2	20	0.5	10	30
	Tetrahydrothiophene	0.1	5	50	0.5	20	60
	Cyclohexanone	0.1	6	60	0.5	15	50
	Styrene	0.1	5	50	0.5	20	60
	Fuel	20	100	800	10	40	150
	Mineral Oil	100	1000	5000	20	200	600

[Reference:M R G Taylor and R A N McLean. IWEM Journal August 1992]

Appendix 4. A guide to the most common contaminants

Listed below is information on some of the more commonly found contaminants.

Arsenic
Arsenic compounds are poisons by inhalation or ingestion. Acute arsenic poisoning from ingestion can cause nausea, vomiting and diarrhoea. Chronic arsenic poisoning can result in damage to the liver, blood, nervous system and kidneys.

Asbestos
Inhalation of asbestos fibres can cause cancers and mesothelioma. Blue Asbestos has the most serious impacts on health.

Cadmium
Cadmium compounds are poisons by ingestion and have been shown to cause lung cancer by inhalation.

Chromium
Ingestion or skin contact may lead to irritation and inflammation of the nose and upper respiratory tract, burns to the skin and kidney damage.

Copper
Acute exposure to copper may lead to irritation to eyes, nose and throat; chills, fever, aches and chest tightness. Repeated high exposure may lead to liver damage.

Cyanides
Cyanide in the form of thiocyanates may lead to skin eruptions and rashes, dizziness, weakness, cramps, nausea, vomiting, mild or severe disturbances of the nervous system, diarrhoea and hypothyroidism.

Lead
Lead compounds may be poisons by ingestion and are a suspected carcinogen of lungs and kidneys. Ingestion or inhalation of lead causes a wide range of problems including anaemia, malaise, headaches, paralysis, hallucinations, nervous system problems and brain damage (diminished IQ) in children.

Mercury
High levels of exposure can cause chest pains and pulmonary edema (the build up of fluid in the lungs) which may lead to death. Repeated exposure may lead to kidney diseases and mental health problems.

Methane
Methane is explosive at levels of 5-15 per cent by volume of air. Government guidance recommends that buildings be evacuated if the level of methane rises above 1 per cent. Methane is also a 'greenhouse gas' and therefore contributes to the threat of climate change.

Nickel
Nickel compounds are poisons and carcinogens by inhalation. Ingestion of nickel compounds can cause intestinal disorders, convulsions and asphyxia. They can cause dermatitis through skin contact.

Phenols (Phenolic Compounds)
Ingestion of phenols can cause burning of the mouth and throat, abdominal pains, nausea, vomiting and diarrhoea, headache, dizziness, weakness. Damage to the central nervous system can lead to coma and death from respiratory failure. Skin contact may lead to corrosion, burns and dermatitis. Phenol contamination of water supplies can cause diarrhoea and mouth sores.

Polycyclic Aromatic Hydrocarbons (PAHs)
A growing number of PAHs have been shown to be carcinogenic in animals and it is recommended by the International Agency for Research on Cancer that they be treated as carcinogenic to humans.

Sulphate
Sulphide ingestion may cause irritation to the mouth and throat. Inhalation of sulphur dust can cause thiopneumoconiosis and bronchitis with emphysema over prolonged periods. Sulphides present may react with moisture to form hydrogen sulphide, which is odorous and at high concentrations can be toxic.

Zinc
Zinc compounds can cause throat dryness, generalized aches, chills, nausea and vomiting through inhalation

[Reference: Department of the Environment: Public Registers of Land which may be Contaminated - A Consultation Paper May 1991]

BUYER BEWARE!

Further Reading

Friends of the Earth publishes a large number of leaflets, briefings and reports on a wide range of environmental issues. The following are a selection; for a full list send a stamped addressed envelope to: Publications Catalogue, Friends of the Earth, 56-58 Alma Street, Luton, Bedfordshire LU1 2YZ. You can order these books using the following order form.

L72 **Your drinking water is being polluted.** *50p*
An illustrated booklet which looks at the causes of water pollution and tells you how to find out what's in your own water supply.

L207 **River Pollution: A Sleuth's Guide** *£3.45*
This illustrated book provides a step-by-step guide to spotting river pollution, using information collected by the National Rivers Authority to trace it to its source and reporting the polluters.

L217 **Water Pollution: Finding the Facts**
A more advanced guide to finding out about the local water environment and how to report polluters. It contains advice on water quality information available from the National Rivers Authority, the drinking water companies and other bodies about rivers, tap water, industrial effluent and radioactive pollution.

LBG165 **How to be a friend of the Earth** *£3.45*
An ideal guide for those who are worried about the environment and want to know what they can do to help. It highlights the reasons why we should be concerned in an accessible and straightforward way, and illustrates that personal action means more than just careful shopping. Energy efficiency, gardening, water pollution and recycling are just some of the areas covered by this colourful and popular book.

T275 **Take the Heat off the Planet** *£3.45*
The world is threatened with climate change, largely due to the massive energy use of industrialized countries like Britain. This colourful guide provides practical advice on what individuals can do to turn their concern into positive action. Easy instructions for

achieving significant savings in energy use at home (and on household fuel bills) are combined with vital information on how to help remove the barriers to energy efficiency which currently exist in the UK.

T246 Don't Throw It All Away £3.45
This easy-to-read, illustrated book examines the 'throwaway society'. It looks at what we throw away, the environmental problems caused by creating so much rubbish, and the potential for reuse and recycling.

L201 21 Years of Friends of the Earth £2.50
This booklet charts the development of Friends of the Earth's campaigns and celebrates some of its biggest victories.

L76 Gas Works Sites in London: an Investigation into Contaminated Land £11.00
Identifies 68 sites used in the manufacture of town gas in London which may be contaminated with dangerous chemicals. It outlines the hazards associated with town gas sites and the implications for local authorities.

Informative, illustrated leaflets on:

LBG75	**Waste**	
LBG124	**Recycling**	
LBG206	**Reusable Packaging**	
LBG225	**Water Pollution**	
LBG43	**Air Pollution**	
LBG42	**Acid Rain**	
LBG62	**Peat**	
LBG83	**Energy**	
LBG166	**Energy Efficiency**	
L91	**Nuclear Power**	
L84	**Renewable Energy**	*50p* each

FRIENDS OF THE EARTH
PUBLICATIONS ORDER FORM

HOW TO ORDER Please complete this order form and send with payment to:
Publications Despatch, Friends of the Earth,
56-58 Alma Street, Luton, Beds LU1 2PL.

NB Please write your order clearly giving both title and code
number and enclose payment with your order.

Add on £2 for postage outside the UK (other than EEC)
Postage and packing is included in all prices
Please allow 28 days for delivery

Name Mr/Mrs/Ms/Miss

Address (for delivery)

Postcode   **Daytime telephone number**

Code	Title	Price	Quantity	Total
	Postage and Packing			**Inclusive**
	Donation			
	TOTAL			

Please make cheques payable to FRIENDS OF THE EARTH or complete your
credit card details here: ☐ **Access**   ☐ **Visa**

				expires	

Cardholder's Signature

Cardholder's address (if different from above) _____

_____

*If you do not want to cut out this coupon, please use a photocopy.

I WOULD LIKE TO SUPPORT THE WORK OF FRIENDS OF THE EARTH'S TRUST

Here is my donation of

☐ £100 ☐ £50

☐ £35 ☐ £15

Sum of your choice £ _____

I enclose total £ _____

payable to: *Friends of the Earth Trust Ltd* or debit my Access / Visa no:

Signature _____ Expiry date _____ / _____

Date _____ / _____ / _____

Name _____

Address _____

_____

_____ Postcode _____

Please send an SAE to the Membership Department if you would like information on any of the following:

☐ Legacies

☐ Covenants

☐ Membership of Friends of the Earth Limited

Phone to donate anytime 0582 485 805

Send to: **Friends of the Earth, 56-58 Alma Street, Luton, Beds LU1 2YZ**.

*If you do not want to cut out this coupon, please use a photocopy.

PB 93063001